THE EVOLUTION OF LIFE.....POETRY FROM THE SOUL

KEVIN GRANVILLE JOHNSON

WHAT IS PERSONAL?

YOU

I sit and think of you,
and wonder in my heart,
just how far I've come.
I always imagine, always fantasize about lovemaking with you.
I need you, I want you.
And no matter where you are, I want to be with you.
I'm lonely without you.
I can't imagine my life without you.
And wherever my heart is,
It will always belong to you.

MERRY CHRISTMAS, BABY

Merry Christmas, Baby,
To you I must say,
For bringing joy and happiness my way.
Merry Christmas, Baby,
For times we've shared,
So often spent,
For songs we've enjoyed,
Our souls we well lent.
Merry Christmas, Baby,
For fantasies and dreams that do come true,
For allowing me to become a part of you.
Merry Christmas, Baby,
And now that we have each other to love,
Now that we've been blessed from Heaven above,
Now that the birds so carelessly sing,
And my heartstrings tingle and do such a zing!!!
Because of those things,
I just want to wish you a.....Merry Christmas, Baby!!!

COULD I BE THE ONE?

Could I be the one you fell in love with?
Could I be the one who makes you feel good inside?
The one who makes you sing?
Could I be the one?
Could I be the one your heart misses, when I'm not around?
The one you yearn so hard for? The one you desire?
Could I be the one? The one for you?
Could I be?

REASONS

You give me reasons to love you.
Because of your gentleness,
Because of your kindness,
Because of the little things you do.
Because you make me feel like I'm a part of your life. A part of you.
Because you make me feel special, appreciated and loved.
And because of that, these are the reasons that I LOVE YOU.

THE SEARCH IS OVER

The Search Is Over.....
Trying to find a love of my own.
Someone whom I could spend some time with,
Grow old with.
The Search Is Over.....
It's been like a roller coaster ride, up and down, high and low.
The Search Is Over.....
I've been pushing myself, just to find a love.
When all it does is cause me even greater pain.
Because there's no one there. So now I'm leaving it all alone.
No more chasing dreams or fantasies.
This is my life's destiny. To be alone.
Because.....The Search Is Over.

MR. BLUES MAN (A TRIBUTE TO MY FATHER, K.C. MATTOX, SR.)

Hey Mr. Blues Man? What's your song today?
Hitting those cords on the guitar, blowing tunes on your harmonica,
With those lyrics that tell the story.
How's your life doing?

Hey Mr. Blues Man? You've got a wife and kids.
On the go especially on the weekends.
Playing at your gigs, making the ladies go CRAZY.
They're making them eyes at you.
Hey Mr. Blues Man? How's your life doing?

Hey Mr. Blues Man, They say you ain't 'bout nothing,
'Cause you got your own thang going.
Ain't kissing no butt, but as long as you got money, you got friends.
But where they at when the money's gone?
Hey Mr. Blues Man? How's your life doing?

Hey Mr. Blues Man, Show Them You The Man!
Don't make no difference if they like you or not!
Show them you got backbone! That you can stand! That you don't need them!
Keep playing and singing the blues, to your hearts content.
You make your family proud! You do what you feel and how you feel!
Stand tall!
Hey Mr. Blues Man? How's your life doing?

SO LONG FOR NOW (A TRIBUTE TO MY GRANDFATHER, EDDIE RAY JOHNSON, SR.)

Grandpa.....
It was good to see you after so many years.
The little boy you once knew grew into a man, responsible and sincere. The many times we talked about life and growing up, about marriage and kids, about building a life and such.
Remembering the days when we went fishing or doing household chores, no matter what the day held, we were never bored.
The smell of fresh cooked fish, the aroma filled the room.
Or watching sports or game shows from morning 'til noon.
I miss you much, even though we live in different parts,
No matter what the circumstance, you will always remain in my heart.
Rest In Peace.

GRANDMA (A TRIBUTE TO MY GRANDMOTHER, ELIZABETH JOHNSON)

I didn't know, I just found out that you are no longer here.
That it's all over, your life is no more.
I didn't know why they kept it from me.
They tried to hide it from me.
I don't think it's fair.
Didn't they know how much I cared?
Now it's over. You are with Grandpa.
Walking through Heaven's doors.
At rest, at peace. I miss you.
I love you. I hope you know that.
I hope that you can still hear me.....Spiritually.
Goodbye Grandma.....Rest In Peace.

LOVE

Been searchin' for so long for love.
Lookin' to fall head over heels.
Searchin' for romance, for excitement, for ecstasy.
But could never find it in anyone I would meet.
They all seemed to shallow, arrogant, so into themselves and their own needs.
But LOVE does not come in the form of a body, or a certain shape or figure.
Real love comes from the heart. It is something you can feel.
It is unconditional.
It can be tested and tried and maybe even tempted.
And yet you can still feel the full affect of it–LOVE.
No matter how wrong you are, or how bad you are, real LOVE will find you, and follow you to the ends of the earth.
Because LOVE asks no questions. It just is...plain and simple...LOVE.

I MISS YOU

I miss you.
I miss your touch and tender kiss.
No one else makes me feel the way you did.
I miss you.
I want you back.
I want the love that we once shared and cherished so tenderly.
I want back the times we spent together.
The lovemaking.....the magic.
Your gentle way of caressing me.
I miss you deeply and I want you back.

REMEMBER WHEN.....

Looking back I can remember all the good times here.

I can remember all the times me and my good friends got together for parties or gatherings.

I can remember what it was like to stay up in the wee hours of the night. Playing cards, laughing and joking, listening to some good ole "Soul Music". I even remember the Holidays, Thanksgiving, when the Turkey was a buffet at the dinner table.

Framed with people standing in line waiting to cut a piece of that white or dark meat.
Or even at Christmas time, shopping for a tree to place in the window for all to see.
Trimmings with lights and glitter and an Angel at the top as a finale.
Or even shopping for Christmas presents for your loved ones.

Seeing the surprised look on their faces when they opened their gifts. Or even the New Year's Eve Party when everyone just gathered together to "Dance" in the New Year, not even knowing what the outcome of that same year would be. But we kept the faith, knowing that we would survive whatever obstacle came our way.   Remember When.....

BAD CHOICES

Sometimes in our lives we struggle constantly to make the best of our lives. To become better people, to enrich our lives. But no matter how hard we try, or no matter how hard we try to avoid them, we often end up making.....Bad Choices. But just because we make Bad Choices, does not mean we are ignorant people, or unaware of what's going on around us, it just simply let's us know that we didn't pay close attention to our facts. That somehow our understanding was clouded by what we thought we knew. Making Bad Choices does not mean we cannot learn from our mistakes. We can actually learn a lesson from all the times we fell flat on our faces. This is actually the experience life gives us. So as we grow older we develop wisdom and knowledge. To help us to look forward to a rewarding future.

THANK YOU

Thank You to my parents for giving me my start.
Thank You to my brothers and sisters who shared my sorrows and troubles.
Thank You to my friends who look out for me and encourage me.
Thank You to those who keep me in their prayers, for prayer is the key that opens every door.
Thank You to those who were here, but are now gone, who have touched my life in some familiar way.
And Thank God, who above all, gives me the strength and courage, wisdom and knowledge, and guidance to run this race with patience.
To meet life's challenges and in keeping the faith.
Thank You.

FRIENDS

The friends we meet should last us a lifetime.
The one's who give us insight on what we need to do to improve our lives. Or the ones who make us smile when we are down and out.
The ones who encourage us.
The ones who have a strong affect on our lives.
The ones who help us see life in a more positive manner.
The ones who have our best interest at heart.
The ones who believe in us.
The ones who help us to stand tall with our chests out, and to help us meet life's challenges and demands.
These are the ones we can call our friends.

WHAT KEEPS A MAN WRITING?

What Keeps A Man Writing?
The ability that God has given him.
The gift to share with all people, all races, the knowledge in giving and sharing.

What Keeps A Man Writing?
His desire to want to learn new things.
To create a passageway for others to receive wisdom and knowledge, of what he has learned in times passed.

What Keeps A Man Writing?
His thoughts, His experiences, His life, What he knows, What he is unsure of. What is past, What is present, The future.
Because he has been given the gift of expression, to uncover and to unfold, all the mysteries in his mind and in his lifetime.

LAST NIGHT

Last Night was incredible.
Like being held captive on a desert island
With someone who is extremely captivating.

Last Night lit the fire to a burning flame of desire and ecstasy.
Two people who exchanged souls.
Two people who shared the art of Lovemaking.
You and I opened up a world filled with new possibilities and joyous pleasures.
Who can blame us for wanting more?

ONCE IN A LIFETIME

Once In A Lifetime,
You meet someone who is your soulmate.
Someone who comes along and makes you feel appreciated, wanted, and loved.
Once In A Lifetime, Someone comes along and makes you laugh, makes you
smile, turns your world inside out.
Once In A Lifetime, Someone comes along and makes you feel like you are the
only two people in the world.
Once In A Lifetime, Two people fall helplessly in love with one another.
Once In A Lifetime,
Two people share a magnificent bond, one that cannot be broken.
Once In A Lifetime, Two people share the same song of love and being together
forever. Once In A Lifetime, Two hearts become one.
Memories are treasured. Absent hearts grow fonder.
Tears become joy. But this only happens.....Once In A Lifetime.

THE SENSITIVE MAN

He cries.
He smiles.
He feels joy.
He knows pain.
Sometimes he's happy.
Sometimes he's sad.
We call him THE SENSITIVE MAN.
He loves hard.
He hates just a little.
He is spiritual.
He is emotional.
Some feel his sensitivity.
Others think he is strange.
But he is just A SENSITIVE MAN.

PROBLEMS

Problems.
Everybody has them.
Everybody deals with them differently.
There is no escape from them.
They are a part of your life.
You try to handle them the best way you know how.
You try to fix them, You try to correct them.
You wonder does the situation get any better.
You wonder do "Problems" ever cease?
Or as long as there is life, will they always be around?
Who doesn't have any problems?
Let him speak now or forever hold his peace.

IN ANOTHER'S ARMS

You held me and kissed me and made me feel joy,
A truth about the matter that should never be told.
Although I find pleasure in my baby's charm,
It's almost magical what you find.....In Another's Arms.

My mind wanders for this short pleasurable time.
For that brief sensual moment we shared.
You touched me, you loved me, you showed me you cared.
There will never be another chance where I could be done harm,
Since I know I have a place to hide.....In Another's Arms.

I can't seem to fight this feeling that has overshadowed my thoughts,
That has me wondering and contemplating the things I ought not.
And even though Heaven moves when my baby shows her charm,
It doesn't even compare when you're making love...In Another's Arms.

WHAT IS EMOTIONAL?

IT RAINED LAST SUMMER

It rained last Summer,
My plans were ruined,
I had no idea what fate had in store or even what I was doing.
My heart skipped a beat, knowing we would be together soon.
A kiss or a smile,
Just to take away my pain or gloom.

It rained last Summer,
But from a distance I heard your despairing cry.
I felt your tears within me and thought to myself "Why?"
We should be together, apart is no excuse.
Bonds should not be broken, ties should not be loosed.
You share what I have, I will give to you my all,
In the Winter, Spring, Summer and Fall.
Whenever it rains, I will think of you.
Sweet love from me to you.

SENSITIVE TEARS

I cry sensitive tears, because I have sensitive heart.
I'm a sensitive man, right from the start.
If you cut me I bleed, if you hurt me I break.
If you lie then I cry, these are the breaks.
I'm a sensitive man, with a great big heart.
Who only want to love, right from the start.

THE RAIN

Gray clouds fill the skies.
There's a light sweet scent in the air.
The Rain.
Water falls from the sky almost like a water faucet.
It's trickling down over your body, you're wet.
The Rain.
It's cold, yet it's sensual, the atmosphere almost romantic.
You almost feel like singing.
The Rain.
Light your fireplace, cuddle in front of it.
Enjoy Sparkling Cider, make love, all the affects of.....
The Rain.

SOMETHING SO UNEXPECTED

Something so unexpected.
Something that feels right.
That gave me another chance to bring love back into my life.
Something I can't see,
But only know that it's real.
That something so unexpected is love.

A STAR*

I wished upon a star, to follow where you are,
To make my dreams come true, to love someone like you.
To stay right by my side, to make my fears subside.
To love and believe, to give and receive.
To have and to hold, to shine as pure gold.
Because I believed, that you I received,
A star twinkles in the night throughout eternity.

LOVE IS A LOSING GAME

Love Is A Losing Game, no matter how you play it, the outcome is still the same.
You open up yourself and give away your heart, just to have the other rip it
apart. You try to be cool knowing that it hurts, but deep down inside you feel
like such a fool.
If you had been wise and knew from the start, that it was all just a game, but
what you played was your heart.
It's not that you win, that's not how you play the game, your emotions ran high,
but still it's just the same.
That no matter how hard you try to gain, the reality of it is that.....
Love Is Just A Losing Game.

LOVE SPEAKS THE SAME LANGUAGE
Those butterflies in your stomach.
Listening to those love songs on the radio.
Your mind wanders, you are lost in romantic thoughts.
You blush a lot, you start to glow, you're starry-eyed.
You become an emotional wreck, you can't think straight.
Your time is spent thinking of her. You're buying flowers and candy.
You're looking at expensive wedding rings.
Your dreams are of the two of you being alone together.
You suddenly find yourself taking long walks on the beach and singing in the rain.
Because somehow, believe it or not, you've fallen in love because...
Love Speaks The Same Language.

A HEART FILLED WITH LOVE
I'm just a guy whose heart is filled with love.
Who's never given a chance to experience true love.
They walk out, As I walk in.
And somehow I know that we will never meet again.
It's easy to say "I Love You", but even harder to prove it.
Who wants a guy that loves too much?
So sometimes I just spend time alone, collecting my thoughts, and wondering when my time will come.
My eyes are red from crying so much, because when you're hurting, what else is there to do?
As the day grows evening into the night the moon shines above,
I'm just a guy sitting here alone, a body whose Heart Is Filled With Love.

RUMOURS

People always seem to enjoy listening to or saying something about other peole even if they know it's not true.

*****Rumours*****

They laugh at you behind your back, grin in your face and then have the nerve to say "We Cool" or "You My Boy", but it doesn't ease the pain that they have caused you.

*****Rumours*****

Sometimes we want to end it all, be transparent into non-existence. You plot, you plan to take your own life, but then you sit and wonder...."Is it worth it?" The Rumours have left you in a state of anger and disappointment.

*****Rumours*****

Will they ever end? Will they ever cease?

Will people one day realize that rumours are vicious? childish? hurtful? painful?

Is it that much fun to humiliate someone even to the point where they don't want to exist? Think about it.

There's a real person behind those vicious*****Rumours*****

LONELY

He knows a lot of people, yet he is lonely.

He is loved by few, hated by many.

Just dealing with being lonely.

He is very quiet and reserved most of the time.

Few people understand him, many don't even try to get to know him.

He is often misunderstood.

His tears are like a heavy burden, like a weight on his shoulders when he cries.

His pain is constant. He is lonely.

Sometimes he is joyous, other times he carries sorrows.

No one to turn to or no one to trust.

So many cut-throats and backstabbers.

His mind is always clicking, thinking of ways to escape his pain.

He hides in memory of "Once Upon A Time",

When he was happy, when he felt loved.

He's just a man whom no matter how things turn out,

He will always be LONELY.

PASSION CRIES

Sensual moves, erotic touches, doth my soul cries out.
Endless dreams, waterfall streams,
While Passion Cries.
Sweet kisses, gentle touches, eyes that speak my name.
Raindrops fall, a sweet dove calls,
While Passion Cries.
My heart skips a beat, your presence I've felt.
My solitude hindered secretly.
A lit candle, a warm fireplace.
A glass of sweet champagne.
Shining stars and their galaxies afar.
Set off.....While Passion Cries.

MR. NICE GUY

He was the one who gave you his heart and soul and just walked away without a word or a notion to defend himself.

That's him.....Mr. Nice Guy.

He's the one whose hurt by so called friends walking around with a dagger or two in his back, bleeding helplessly, showing one big scar, feeling the wound from front to back.

That's him.....Mr. Nice Guy.

He's the guy whose constantly talked about by his peers, often misunderstood, laughed at and ridiculed.

Always forgotten, never thought about, to the point of non-existence.

That's him.....Mr. Nice Guy.

He's the one whose soul cries out to be loved, whose spirit is often broken because his emotions are toyed with.

Because people love to hurt him. Because he's sensitive to others needs, while his are never being met.

He's the guy who is always lied on and mistreated because people get a jolt out of hurting his feelings.

He's the one who strives to be happy, but is constantly sad. He's the one with no one to count on, on one to depend on, no one to trust in. He's the one who's afraid to fight back because he knows he might lose. He's the one who dies slowly. God help him.

He's Mr. Nice Guy.

IT'S NOT FAIR

It's Not Fair that my last memory of you was in a wooden box, lifeless.

It's Not Fair that after three and a half years that passed by, we had to say our goodbyes at your homegoing.

It's Not Fair that the last time I remember seeing you physically was at a former funeral.

It's Not Fair that the people involved in your murder, got away with murder. It should have been them who paid the price.

It's Not Fair that your children are left motherless, that your family is suffering behind the situation these two young men put them in.

It's Not Fair that I didn't have one last chance to say "I Love You".

It's Not Fair that what they did to you, everybody else had to suffer.

It's Not Fair.

Aunt Maxine Hall..........Rest In Peace...........October 1993

WHAT IS LOVE?

What is love and why does it hurt?

Why can't it be something pleasant rather than painful?

Who created love so that you can feel it's pain, it's tension, it's poison? Why does it affect the heart so? What makes it so emotional?

What makes the heart yearn for more of it? Even though it can be stressful? Aggravating? Painful?

How do you heal a wounded heart shot by the arrows cupid called "Love?"

How will you get through the fear of a heart being broken by love?

Is it something sweet? Or should we call it bitter?

Is love our friend? Or your finest enemy?

Could love be good to the soul, the body, bone and marrow?

Or could love be a poison killing you, leaving you all alone?

Some say it's a good thing because whoever finds it, finds a treasure.

Others say it's a waste of time, a waste of sheer pleasure.

But no matter what the outcome, Love has its arrows.

Waiting to poke you through the heart, through the bone and marrow. Can you explain to me simply what love is?

IF

If love was air, I could breathe freely.
If love was a plane, I could fly non-stop.
If love was a river, there could be no depth.
If love was a mountain, it could reach sky high.
If love was a rainbow, so many could see the affect.
If love was a whisper, it would be sweet to the ear.
If love could carry me back and forth across a deep blue sea,
Then there would always be just enough space for you and me.

I WONDER

There is sex, and there is love.
What makes the two different?
There are those who want to be loved.
Who want and need to feel love.
And there are those who just lust constantly.
One person is never enough for them.
How do you get through your day, knowing that you were something that was lusted after, rather than loved?
Can your heart and mind erase the pain of being hurt?
Can you overcome? Can you move on?
Maybe one day the other person will fall in love and the same thing will happen to them.
Who knows? I Wonder.

WHY?

I wonder, why won't you love me, the way you love him?
What makes him so special?
How is it that no matter how hard I try, I can't seem to forget you?
Even though I need you, I want you.
I try to forget you but I can't.
Memories of that special night we had together comes to the surface.
When will you love me?

IF LOVE MUST GO

If love must go, then let it go.
If love must leave, then leave it there.
If a heart is broken or torn to pieces, why try to mend it?
If love has a cure for the pain left behind, then where can I find it?
Who knows how to cure pain love left behind?
Does real love exist?
Or is it a temporary feeling for most?
Can I survive this? Can I get through this?
Is there another one who shares the same feelings or emotions as I?
If love must go, then simply let it go.

PEACE OF MIND

A troubled world, full of issues and mishaps, turmoil and hatred.
Living in a world that degrades the rights of mankind.
A world that kills innocence and shows no regard for the living.
All I ask for during this crisis is some.....PEACE OF MIND.

DEATH

It is pre-destined, pre-planned.
Whether we want to accept it to not.
It will eventually happen to all of us.

We don't like to think about it, nor do we like to talk about it.
It is something that we push far back into our minds.
Almost to the point of forgetfulness.

Of course, Death is not a pleasant thing.
Nor really is it an evil thing.
It is just a time in our lives, where we come to an end of a long journey. The Journey Of Life.

Death ends here on earth.
But it is really the beginning of a new life.....Eternal Life.
God is just preparing us to come and live with Him.
Actually, Death is the end of one life and the start of another.

Death.....Don't be afraid!

Dedicated to Mrs. Amy Watts (In Remembrance of Mr. Charles Watts).

WHAT IS SPIRITUAL?

HE IS.....

He Is.....
Wisdom and knowledge.
He knows all and sees all.
His love is unconditional.
He knows all about you. He cares about you.
He is concerned about your well being.
He only wants the best for you.
For all His children.
He Is.....
The reason you exist.
There is no one else like Him.
He Is.....God.

BE TRUE TO YOURSELF

Be True To Yourself.
Remember this I say.
No matter what happens, you'll get through each day.
Friends come and friends go, through your circle of life.
This is one thing you've got to know.
Be True To Yourself.
Let your heart be your guide.
Take nothing personal, take it all in stride.
Step high.
Never look low.
For no one is perfect.
Stay True To Yourself.

THE CALLED

You are The Called.
A vessel chosen by God.
To do as He commands, in doing His will.
You are The Called, who stands alone, without many friends.
You are The Called, according to His purpose.
He has a plan for your life that will be carried out.
You are The Called.
In spite of your enemies.
You stand tall with your head held high.
There's no need to worry, or no need to fear, because God is with you. To see
you through every trial and tribulation.
He will look out for you.
He has chosen you among many others.
You were created by Him, for Him.
To Worship and Praise Him.
Many demands to be met, but you can do it!
Because you are The Called.....His Child!

RISE ABOVE IT!

When people talk bad about you and try to do things to tear you down,
    RISE ABOVE IT!

When people try to hurt you and turn other people against you,
    RISE ABOVE IT!

When people smile in your face and throw daggers in your back,
    RISE ABOVE IT!

When so-called friends turn their backs on you, walk away from you,
    RISE ABOVE IT!

When people have lied on you and set traps for you to try to fall into,
When rumors are spreading around about you, just to keep you down,
    RISE ABOVE IT!

When life just sometimes doesn't seem fair and you feel like giving up! Don't throw in the towel, hold on with everything you've got and simply......RISE ABOVE IT!

WHO KNOWS?

Who knows what tomorrow holds as you lay your head down to sleep, as
mysteries unfold and each plot deepens knowing every burden that you bear?
Every test and trial is not given to hurt you, but is a
measurement of strength and faith in this day and time.
Use wisdom to the best of your ability to maintain the situation.
Peace.

WHAT IS VICTORIOUS?

THE MAN THAT I AM

It takes a strong woman, a loving woman, one who loves and fears God, to raise a strong and independent man. This comes from generations of strong God-fearing women, such as generations before.

Before you, (my own mother), was grandma Janey, and her mother, and her mother's mother and so on.

Women have actually been in charge when it came to raising the children in their families as far as the whippings and punishments and upbringing of the children were concerned.

I am not excluding the men per-say, but alongside every man is definitely a good woman, and you need to count yourself worthy!

I thank God that I am the man that I am today.

Not only because God has blessed me with one good, strict, stern, patient, faithful mother, but for the history and generations of the women in our families behind that. Thank you for the whippings, the scoldings, the punishments, and the church fellowships. For had it not been for some of those things, where would your own children be? (Kevin, K.C. Jr., Alicia, Gabrielle, and Jason).

This seed of faithfulness passed down to this present time, would be accounted for in your grandchildren's future.

THANKS MOM!

Love.....Kevin
P.S. You are never forgotten!

FEARS

We all have them.
They seem to affect our lives in the most peculiar way.
They are real.
How do you deal with them? How do you handle them?
Are they all a part of a sub-conscious imagination we have in the back of our minds? Or is it a forewarning to keep us prepared?
What are they?
Where do they come from?
Are we strong enough to deal with them?
Be prepared, Stay aware.

MOVING ON

Moving On past life's problems is what I'm trying to do.
Making adjustments and making sacrifices.
Sometimes it's hard, but once you set your mind to it, you can do it!
Step by step, I am determined to create a better life for myself and for my future. To elevate, to enhance, to excel every part of my being into advancing through wisdom and knowledge.
Constant craving, for more of what life has to offer which gives me more of an opportunity in.....Moving On.

SILVER LINING

People are always talking about the many times they've been hurt or how often they've been stood up or how their friends have deceived them. The world we live in seems to be one of heartache and pain.
But we must remember, behind every dark cloud, there is a.....
Silver Lining. Reach for your Silver Lining. That's where the rain ends.

LIFE IS A TEST

Life Is A Test.
It's up to you to pass or fail.
Life Is A Test.
Through every meadow, through every trail.
No matter how hard the problem, it should be easy to solve.
Keep your answers to yourself, let no one see your strategies to survive. For all who live in this life, don't play fair.
They don't play by the rules. They will steal what you have to gain great for themselves. But in the end they look like such fools.
For you should live the truth and never a lie, just as the bible states:
"A TOOTH FOR A TOOTH, AN EYE FOR AN EYE."
But you don't survive by getting over, nor do you win by stepping over others.
But you give your heart to let other's see, that no matter what pain or agony, you'll fight fair, for in the end this test will show.....
THE REAL YOU!

I'M BLACK AND I'M PROUD!

I'm Black and I'm Proud!
Regardless of what society has said about me, or done to me,
I Stand Proud!
I'm Black and I'm Proud!

I'm no lesser of a person that what other men have made me out to be. I will overcome because I Stand Proud!
I'm Black and I'm Proud!

I'm not a drug dealer, nor a dope fiend, nor a purse snatcher.
I'm not a hooker, nor a rapist, nor a child molester. I'm not poor.
I don't live in poverty, I don't lack knowledge.

I am a Black man, who lives in a world created by society to tear down what we have struggled so long to build.
A future for our people, our children, ourselves.

We are not less than, but equal to. We are not lower than, but more than above. We do have rights. And even though others treat us differently, or look at us strangely, even though we must fight to build a better tomorrow, even though men say that we would never amount to anything, no we could never do anything, even though we are laughed at and ridiculed, nevertheless, I will stand tall.....

Because I'm Black and I'm Proud!

THE WHITE EAGLE

The White Eagle.
He soars, He glides.
High above the atmosphere, High above his nest.
He sees, He hears, He knows, He keeps flying.
For he is in control of his DESTINY!

DEAR GOD

DEAR GOD.....
Only you know why there are so many murders among your people. Only you
know why there is so much rebellion and hatred in a world you created. Only
you know why sin has overtaken the heart of man to make him do evil.
But in the midst of it all, I seek for perfect peace. Yet still the storms are raging
high. But in the midst of the storm, work your perfect work In me. Let your will
be done in my life.....DEAR GOD.

THROUGH A CHILD'S EYES

Through A Child's Eyes, they see no hurt, no sorrow.
Through A Child's Eyes, the world is one with them.
Through A Child's Eyes, they see no color. There is no racism.
Everyone to them is the same.
Created Equally.
Through A Child's Eyes.

LIFE IS....

LIFE IS.....The most precious gift God has given to us. How will you live it?

Sometimes we take life for granted. Sometimes we feel that we are cheated when life does not give us what we want, when we want it. We fail to realize that the gift of life is given with the opportunity for you to appreciate what you can do with it. You can affect your own life or even someone else's life by what you choose to do with it.

LIFE IS.....A mystery to us all. We don't know exactly how long our life span reaches or how long we are destined to remain on this earth, but we have an opportunity to leave a mark, to make history, and that's what life is really about. A sourceof life being passed on from one generation to the next, from decade to decade, century to century.

We must remember that.....**LIFE IS.....**

JOY, PAIN, LAUGHTER, SORROW, LIVING, DYING, GROWING UP, BEING PULLED DOWN, LOVE, HATRED, IGNORANCE, AND INTELLIGENCE.

And no matter who you are, or where you are, or where you live, LIFE has a name and a place for everyone. So do yourself a favor, don't cheat yourself. Live your LIFE to the fullest of your enjoyments.....
WITH NO REGRETS.

MY THOUGHT PROCESS

WHAT IS.....EMOTIONAL?
Something or Someone who causes you to react to something in a sentimental or moody way. Something that connects with the heart.

WHAT IS.....PERSONAL?
Something that deals with that person as a whole. Something that is completely private and confidential. Something to do with just that certain individual or that individuals needs.

WHAT IS.....SPIRITUAL?
Something connecting with the elements of the earth. Something that connects the Mind, Body, Soul and Spirit to the heart of God.
One who is sensitive towards spirituality.

WHAT IS.....VICTORIOUS?
One who can overcome difficult and intense situations. One who is persevering. One who can stand through the test of time.

WHAT IS LIFE? MY THOUGHT PROCESS SAYS THAT LIFE IS.....
~EMOTIONAL~
~PERSONAL~
~SPIRITUAL~
~VICTORIOUS~

GOD BLESS YOU ALL!

KEVIN GRANVILLE LAWRENCE JOHNSON

THIS BOOK IS DEDICATED TO THE MEMORY OF:

MR. AND MRS. LAWRENCE GRAY, SR.
MR. AND MRS. EDDIE JOHNSON, SR.
MAXINE HALL
CYNTHIA GRAY
HELEN JACKSON
TODD ANTHONY RODRIGUEZ
RUBY NELL JEFFRIES
RENEE HUTCHINGS-WYATT
LAWANA WALLER
DR. RUTH LANGSTON (HAMILTON MEMORIAL CHURCH OF GOD IN CHRIST)
BISHOP LONNIE C. PATTON (JERUSALEM CHURCH OF GOD IN CHRIST)

THANK YOU'S.....

I WOULD LIKE TO THANK MY LORD AND SAVIOUR JESUS CHRIST FOR
EMPOWERING ME WITH THE GIFT AND THE ABILITY TO WRITE. THE GIFT OF
EXPRESSION.
MY FAMILY.....
MR. AND MRS. K.C. AND JOYCE MATTOX, SR.,
MY SIBLINGS....KALVIN CHARLES, PATTY, K.C. JR., ALICIA, GABRIELLE, AND
JASON
              AND THEIR FAMILIES.
JOE AND FLORENCE/GARDNEIL/NEICY/TYGEE/STEVIE (MY SAN JOSE CLAN).
THE BROOKS FAMILY: SAM AND JOCEE/WORTHY AND DORIS/DAISY AND
NOVA/JEROME AND JOYCE/VAN/TAMMY/DANA.
MR. AND MRS. WILLIE AND CAROL JOHNSON/ THE JOHNSON FAMILY.
MR. AND MRS. DWIGHT AND KIM BARNETT AND FAMILY/ THE BARNETT FAMILY.
MR. AND MRS. LAWRENCE AND KAROL GRAY JR, AND FAMILY/ THE GRAY
FAMILY.
MS. BILLIE JO FINNEY/THE BESS FAMILY/THE CHATMAN FAMILY.
PASTOR AND MRS. SCOTT AND KRISTY BROOKS AND FAMILY.
CHANGED LIFE CHURCH MINISTRIES AND STAFF.

MR. KEN SIMONTON/MR. JOE FIAME/GINA FIAME/ANTHONY FIAME/CARLTON WALSTON/RANDALL GORY/TYRONE AND ANDREA TAYLOR.
CORRINE HENDERSON AND FAMILY/ MR. ALEX (MARCELLIS) HARRIS
MR. AND MRS. ANTONIO HUERTA AND FAMILY/MR. CALVIN DUNN/MR. NIKOLAS DUNN/MR. OTHELL DUNN (THE DUNN GENERATION).

I WOULD ALSO LIKE TO THANK ALL THOSE WHO CONTINUE TO SUPPORT ME, ENCOURAGE ME, AND CONSISTENTLY PRAY FOR ME AS I WORK ON EACH AND EVERY PROJECT. THANK YOU.
GOD BLESS YOU.
EVOLUTION OF LIFE.....POETRY FROM THE SOUL   KEVIN JOHNSON

WELL LADIES AND GENTLEMEN, HE'S DONE IT AGAIN! THIS IS MR. JOHNSON'S SECOND PROJECT,
"EVOLUTION OF LIFE...POETRY FROM THE SOUL".
HIS FIRST PROJECT, "TELL ME, WHAT'S ON YOUR MIND?" COMPLETELY SOLD OUT WHICH BECAME A BIG SUCCESS IN THE EAST BAY/CONTRA COSTA AREA. MR. JOHNSON STATES:

"THIS IS A CONTINUATION OF THE FIRST PROJECT, "TELL ME, WHAT'S ON YOUR MIND?" WHICH IS BROKEN DOWN INTO FOUR CATEGORIES....

WHAT IS PERSONAL?
WHAT IS EMOTIONAL?
WHAT IS SPIRITUAL?
WHAT IS VICTORIOUS?

AND SHARES WITH THE PUBLIC AN EVEN MORE INTIMATE SIDE OF MYSELF. WRITING IS AND WILL ALWAYS BE A PASSION OF MINE. IT'S A PART OF ME, AND WILL ALWAYS BE. I'M VERY APPRECIATIVE AND THANKFUL THAT GOD HAS BLESSED ME WITH SUCH A GREAT GIFT.....
THE GIFT OF EXPRESSION. I AM ALSO GRATEFUL TO ALL MY FAMILY AND FRIENDS FOR THEIR SUPPORT AND PRAYERS DURING THIS PROJECT. THANK YOU

AND GOD BLESS YOU ALL!"

THIS IS ONLY THE BEGINNING FOR MR. JOHNSON WHO HAS ALREADY COMPLETED THREE OTHER PROJECTS NOT YET RELEASED TO THE PUBLIC. LET'S WISH HIM WELL AS HE CONTINUES TO SHARE HIS ASPIRATIONS AND DREAMS TO THE WORLD.

COMMENTARIES.....

"TRAIN UP A CHILD IN THE WAY HE SHOULD GO, AND WHEN HE IS OLD, HE WILL NOT DEPART FROM IT." PROVERBS 22:6
THIS PROVERB IS SO BEFITTING TO OUR SON, FOR HE'S NEVER STRAYED FROM GOD AND THE MORAL VALUES TAUGHT TO HIM AS A CHILD. FROM THE TIME OF HIS BIRTH, GOD'S DIRECTION FOR HIM WAS ALREADY SET IN PLACE.

GROWING UP, KEVIN HAS ALWAYS DISPLAYED SUCH QUALITIES OF CARE, WARMTH, AND SENSITIVITY AND THESE TRAITS ARE WELL REFLECTED IN BOTH HIS PERSONAL AND PROFESSIONAL LIFE. HIS WRITING REVEALS HIS WIT, EMOTIONS, CHARM, WISDOM, AND SUCH ZEAL FOR LIFE.
IT'S SO AMAZING AS WE LOOK BACK, THIS SOMEWHAT SHY AND SENSITIVE LITTLE BOY
(AND EVEN AS A TEEN AND ENTERING MANHOOD), WHO WOULD CONFIDE IN US AND ASK FOR ADVICE, NOW SHARES HIS OWN THOUGHT PROVOKING PERSPECTIVES ON LIFE, LOVE, AND THE UNESCAPING PROBABILITIES WITH OTHERS IN HIS WRITING.
THANK YOU GOD FOR YOUR GUIDING HAND AND FOR BLESSING US WITH SUCH A GIFTED CHILD WHO IS NOW " A MAN OF STANDARDS".

WE LOVE YOU KEVIN.   DAD AND MOM.

"BY VIRTUE OF HIS PASSION, KEVIN EXUDES A MOHAGANY OF DEEP TEXTURE IN HIS WORDS. RICH IN HIS TONES AND PERSONAL INFLECTIONS OF A LIFE LIVED, THIS BODY OF WORK ILLUMINATES THE PERSONAL VICTORY OF THE ARTIST. THROUGH LIFE, LOVE AND PAIN, THIS IS A WORK THAT CANNOT BE SEPERATED FROM THE CAREFUL CRAFTSMAN THAT IS.....KEVIN JOHNSON."

MR. KENNETH SIMONTON
CHANGED LIFE CHURCH

Whenever You're Away From Me   March 3, 1992

Whenever You're Away From Me,
My heart sings a sad melody,
An offbeat tune.
Whenever You're Away From Me,
Tears seem to be the showers of an everyday awakening.

Whenever You're Away From Me,
The longing and desire and yearning to be with you is just to unreal,
Wanting you, missing you,
Like a giant wall between us, needing to get to you,
Needing to hold you, to tell you how much " I LOVE YOU".
Whenever You're Away From Me,
My world just crumbles,
AND MY LIFE JUST ISN'T THE SAME!

Valentine's Day   **February 14, 1992**

All I can say is that "I Love You!"
It's hard to describe the many ways you make me feel inside.
So much laughter, So much joy and happiness.
But it does not end there. The way you touch me.
The way you hold me. Even the way you kiss me tells me the story of how much
"You" love "Me". Those romantic moments together.
Even the intimacy we share during lovemaking is "magic".
The feeling I get deep down inside when you tell me you love me.
The way your eyes light up when you look at me!
The passion in your tongue and lips when you kiss me.
All of these things bring joy to my every being.
The feeling of impatience I get brought on by my every desire to see you again,
Hold you again, touch you again, the sweet sensation you have left behind,
That when you leave, makes my heart yearn and desire you more.
I can't explain the man I've become since you came into my life.
I feel almost like a teenager, a kid whose first experience with love is like sheer HEAVEN!
All I know is that I Love You, because without "YOU", the "ME" doesn't exist!

Love Knows   **June 1994**

Love Knows, When it is being tested, When it is being tried,
When you must face the truth, When to you someone lied.
Love Knows, Every condition of hurt you must endure,
Peace of mind, contentment, just when you need to be sure.
Love Knows, The passion inside your heart you give away,
Waiting the next moment, Knowing the price you must pay.
Love Knows, Every risk and turn you must face,
Hidden questions, Avoided answers that take up time and space.
Love Knows, The mysteries that lie within the heart,
A deep fascination in which we all play a part.

Paint The Perfect Picture   July 1989
Paint The Perfect Picture of you and me,
A never ending romance.
Sculpt the perfect image of our love being transferred, from one heart to another.
Draw me an outline of what it takes to make an Everlasting Love last and to keep the togetherness of what is called
"The Perfect Couple", and Hang, Frame and Hang it upon the walls for others to see or maybe even envy that there
can be a love so true! A love designed by two can never be tested nor torn apart because Love and Trust are the true ingredients for A STRONG RELATIONSHIP!

Somehow   **July 1995**

Somehow I feel that what is meant to happen will happen.

Mistakes that happen are put aside to make room for new and exciting memories we can share.

Somehow, we found our way back to one another.

Though we may be physically apart from one another, our minds and our thoughts connect with one another.

Somehow I can smell your scent, feel your heartbeat, read your mind, walk inside your dreams,

Converse with you silently in thought, in mind.

Somehow, without even thinking, I know I am on your mind, and in your thoughts.

You keep me privately and discreetly in your heart, where I belong.

What I Want Out Of Love   **November 13, 1994**
What I Want Out Of Love,
Is to be loved completely, not partially.
What I Want Out Of Love,
Is to receive, As I give back to my receiver.
What I Want is to grow and mature,
As you nurture and feed.
What I ask for is little,
Even though I expect very much.
What I Want Out Of Love,
Is to know that even though it may not be forever,
It's good to know that it was almost there.

The Night I Fell In Love   **December 8, 1991**
The Night I Fell In Love all over again,
The Night you made me feel love again,
The Night you told me you loved me,
The Night you held me in your arms,
The Night I saw your tears of joy and happiness,
The Night we made love,
The Night you called me just to hear my voice, and to confide in me,
The Night you made me open up honestly, and to share with you, my most innermost feelings,
The Night you asked me, "Is It A Crime To Fall In Love?"
The Night you came back into my life was.....
THE NIGHT I FELL IN LOVE!

FROM THE AUTHOR'S DESK.....KEVIN JOHNSON

I AM SO THANKFUL AND SO GRATEFUL TO ALL OF THE PEOPLE THAT HAVE SUPPORTED ME AND BELIEVED IN ME AND THIS PROJECT. THIS IS MY SECOND PROJECT IN WHICH I AM VERY PROUD AND VERY EXCITED IN HAVING IT PUBLISHED. THIS LETTER THAT I AM PUTTING TOGETHER IS NOT JUST TO SHOW YOU THAT I LOVE WRITING OR POETRY, BUT IT IS A LETTER OF ENCOURAGEMENT TO ALL THOSE THAT HAVE DREAMS TO DO SOMETHING BIG, BUT NOT SURE WHERE TO START. LET ME BE THE FIRST TO ENCOURAGE YOUR ENDEAVORS AND YOUR DREAMS IN MAKING THEM COME TRUE. HERE IS A LITTLE FOOD FOR THOUGHT:

MY FIRST PROJECT, "TELL ME, WHAT'S ON YOUR MIND?" I STARTED THAT IN 93 AND IT DIDN'T GET PUBLISHED UNTIL 2003. WHY? FIRST BECAUSE I THOUGHT THAT NO ONE WOULD WANT TO READ SOME OF MY MATERIAL. I WASN'T FOR SURE IF I WANTED TO PUT MY MATERIAL OUT THERE FOR OTHERS TO "CRITIQUE". BUT THEN ONE DAY MY COUSIN SAW SOME OF MY MATERIAL AND SPOKE WITH MY MOTHER ABOUT IT AND TOLD HER THAT HE THOUGHT I SHOULD GET IT PUBLISHED. MY MOM HAD CALLED ME AND WE HAD A LONG TALK ABOUT IT. I WAS STILL SOMEWHAT HESITANT, BUT AFTER READING HER SOME OF MY MATERIAL AND SHARING IT WITH OTHER CLOSE FAMILY MEMBERS, I DECIDED TO PUT TOGETHER A BOOK...."TELL ME, WHAT'S ON YOUR MIND?"

IT WASN'T AN EASY JOURNEY. I WAS IN THE PROCESS OF MOVING WHICH SLOWED DOWN MY FUNDS FOR THE PROJECT, MY HOURS HAD WENT FROM FULL-TIME WORK TO PART-TIME WORK, AND ON TOP OF THAT, MY PAY RATE DECREASED. I HAD STOPPED MAKING PAYMENTS ON MY PROJECT AND WAS ACTUALLY READY TO THROW IN THE TOWEL. MY PUBLISHER'S HAD SENT ME A LETTER, CERTIFIED STATING THAT IF I MISSED ANY MORE PAYMENTS, WE WOULD HAVE TO CANCEL THE CONTRACT AND THEY WOULD SEND ME HALF OF THE MONEY BACK FOR THE WRITTEN MATERIAL. I WAS JUST GOING TO LET THEM DO THAT AND JUST SAY "FORGET IT!" BUT MY MOM BELIEVED IN ME AND TOLD ME NOT TO QUIT OR NOT TO GIVE UP. THAT I HAD COME THIS FAR, HALFWAY IN PAYMENTS SO I SHOULD CONTINUE. I REALLY DIDN'T SEE HOW I WAS GOING TO DO ALL OF THAT KNOWING THAT I HAD TO MOVE AND MY FINANCIAL SITUATION WAS VERY POOR. BUT I TOOK HER ADVICE AND CONTINUED TO MAKE PAYMENTS.

A FEW YEARS AFTER THAT, I HAD LOST MY JOB, AND WAS DRAWING UNEMPLOYMENT. I STILL MADE PAYMENTS, BUT MY UNEMPLOYMENT RAN OUT AND I WAS STUCK ON HOW I WAS GOING TO MAKE PAYMENTS TO MY PUBLISHING COMPANY. MY PARENTS BELIEVED IN ME AND SUPPORTED ME EVEN THOUGH THEY KNEW I WAS OUT OF WORK AND THEY KNEW THAT THIS PROJECT WAS VERY IMPORTANT TO ME. THEY WOULD SEND ME MONTHLY CHECKS, NOT TO SPLURGE OR GO OUT SHOPPING (MOM'S WASN'T HAVING IT!), BUT TO HELP WITH THE BILLS AND TO HELP PAY OFF MY PUBLISHING FEES.

WELL HERE'S THE GOOD PART....FINALLY AFTER YEARS OF WAITING AND ANTICIPATING....I RECEIVED A LETTER FROM THE PUBLISHING COMPANY SAYING THAT I ONLY OWED **"ONE MORE PAYMENT"**. I COULDN'T BELIEVE IT. I WAS SO HAPPY THAT THIS PROJECT WAS JUST ABOUT COMPLETED AND READY TO GO INTO PUBLICATION. SO

AFTER THE FINAL PAYMENT, MARCH 2003 IS WHEN UPS RANG MY DOORBELL AND HANDED ME A LITTLE BROWN SLIM BOX WITH THE NAME..."**KEVIN JOHNSON**" ON IT, I KNEW THEN THAT ONCE I OPENED THE BOX, WHAT I HAD WORKED SO HARD FOR AND ANTICIPATED, AND STRUGGLED TO MAKE THIS PROJECT HAPPEN, WHAT I WAITIED MANY YEARS FOR, WAS RIGHT IN THE PALM OF MY HANDS. AND WHEN I FINALLY OPENED THE BOX, I DID I ADMIT, HAD TEARS RUNNING DOWN MY CHEEKS, BECAUSE THERE IT WAS IN BEAUTIFUL BOLD LETTERS, **"TELL ME, WHAT'S ON YOUR MIND?' KEVIN JOHNSON.**

AND NOW I HAVE THE JOY AND PLEASURE OF PRESENTING TO YOU MY SECOND PROJECT IN WHICH I HOPE THAT YOU WOULD ENJOY.....
"THE EVOLUTION OF LIFE.....POETRY FROM THE SOUL". THIS PROJECT IS DEDICATED TO ALL THOSE THAT ARE NOT QUITE SURE WHERE TO START AND NOT QUITE SURE WHICH DIRECTION TO GO. BELIEVE THIS..."**IF I CAN DO IT, SO CAN YOU!**" I HOPE THAT THIS PROJECT GIVES YOU THE STRENGTH AND ENCOURAGEMENT YOU NEED FOR THAT JOURNEY, THOUGHT IT MAY NOT BE AN EASY ONE, BUT THE FINISHED PRODUCT FROM THE WORK THAT YOU HAVE PUT IN AND BELIEVED IN, IS MOST DEFINITELY WORTH THE WAIT.

GOD BLESS YOU ALL.

KEVIN GRANVILLE JOHNSON

In My Heart   **July 1995**

There is song In My Heart, that you have left for me to sing.

A tune that says you are the one I want to be with.

A yearning that pulls from within the depths of my soul, to the heights of my vessels.

A craving of pure desire to sweep you off your feet, into a world of unconditional...PASSION!

To seek, to find, to capture you. To seduce you.

To allow my melody and my song to entice us into a world of unimaginary ecstasy.

To somehow overpower the feeling of excitement and intensity you have left for me....

INSIDE MY HEART!

Whipped Cream   **August 1995**

Flowing like a river from beneath your love canal, comes a surprisingly White, sweet, milky, creamy delight
that sets my desires to a burning flame. Licking your body from head to toe, sucking every drop of your sweat that melts in my mouth like silk cotton candy. The scent of your body, the look in your eyes when I take you in my arms and caress you gently, the results of your love, meeting my love, causes a chemical reaction which explodes into
an odyssey of WHIPPED CREAM.

Baby   **August 1995**

Baby, You and I sharing exotic kisses and uninhibited lovemaking, can make a candle melt down to the lowest
form of sinking sand, slowly swallowing us up in an ecstasy of passion.

As You Are   **August 1995**

The Sun is to the Earth, The Flame that keeps it warm, As You Are to my soul the desire to live.

If love were a shadow, then I would follow you to the ends of the Earth, until you surrendered to my every need.

If wanting you was an everyday chore, then my body would be tired from working its everyday charm, to win you over,

Mind, Body, Soul, and Spirit.

Someone Like You   **September 1995**

Who would have believed Someone Like You,
Could enter my life and take over my heart.
Someone Like You can make me feel like I could soar through the skies and sing harmonious melodies with the birds.
Someone Like You could sleep with me in my dreams, and be my pillow as I awake.
Someone that could cause an excitement just by thinking of them. Someone that could get me all fluttered with excitement just to hear their voice. Someone who makes me yearn just to be near them. Someone who makes my life complete.
Someone Like You, is whom I want to end up with…..
On the other side of ETERNITY!

You and I   **November 1995**

You are someone I love and want to share my life with.
You are the joy inside my tears.
You make my heart skip a beat.
You make me want to sing in the rain.
You make my life worth living.
You put a smile on my face.
You cause an inner glow.
You put me in a romantic mood, just being around you.
You are what I live for.
I want to be your lover.
I want to be your friend.
I want to possess your soul.
I want your love.
I want to be closer to you.
I want to show you the world.
I want you to be mine forever…..throughout Eternity.

Thanksgiving Day Grace (Just For You)   **November 1995**

Since I've met you, I find it hard to believe you were my friend first.
You knew all about me. We've had a hard start trying to become close.
But we never gave up. For me, you were there the most.
My problems increased, my world fell apart.
I had no one to call. It was like a knife in my heart.
But you were always there, waiting in the wings.
With open arms, I felt just like a King.
Your smile was beautiful. It lit up every room.
It took away my sorrow. It took away my gloom.
It's always good to know, that I have someone like you, who loves me unconditionally, and who makes my gray skies Blue.
So don't ever worry, and don't you ever fret,
Because you're the best thing that has happened to me yet.
And when my day is over, and I fall fast asleep,
Remember you're my one and only,
Because my love for you runs deep.

Choices   **August 1992**

In life there are many choices.

Good ones, bad ones.

Ones that make us think about the effect that they will have on our lives for a long time. Choices concerning our life. Our friends. Who we become. What we did, who we are, and how we think. Choices tell us after awhile, where do we go? What goals we must reach. Choices concerning sex, our partners, our life. Our careers, our families. Believe it or not, choices affect just about everything we say and do. So we must carefully examine ourselves. We must decide within ourselves that we are going to make the best possible "CHOICE". Because one mistake might cost us our lives, or even the lives of others around us.

The Creator   **November 1987**
The Earth was Black. He gave it light.
The Sky was empty. He added the moon, the stars and the sun.
The Plateau was empty. He added the sea for the fish and all mammals.
The Ground was empty. He added trees and flowers and decorated them with birds and bees and butterflies.
And then He discovered there was no one to see His marvelous works.
No one to witness His beauty of creation.
So then He created from dust, through the breath of His own life and His own image, MAN, through His ribs, WOMAN, and today they know of…..THE CREATOR.

Honesty   **April 1995**

It comes from within.
It is something that tells others the kind of person you are.
It is something others can feel and see, through your example of living it.
If you allow it, it can be a part of your life, a part of your future.
It tells others that you abide by this rule, that there is no half-stepping.
It is something that is passed on from generation to generation.
It can bring a nation together. It can make the world stand still.
It can make you fall to your knees. It can bring unity, and conquer hatred.
The word alone can cause men to cease war.

Life   **October 1995**
Only for a short time, some live to be 100 years old.
Others are gone too soon. Some even die at birth.
We don't know how long life is, we just live from day to day.
Hoping and praying we would never have to experience the unexpected, suddenly.
Even though you're never prepared, you sit and wonder in the back of your minds.
What is the secret to having a long life? Or does God predestine our life span?
What would life be like if we were to never die? Would our lives be different?
Would we think or act differently? The secret of life will always remain a mystery.
(In Loving Memory of Bridgette Salone).

How I See Myself   **September 1995**

How I See Myself? I see myself as an artist, bringing color and excitement into many lives. As a doctor, helping to ease the pain for many around me.

As a counselor, trying to help those around me solve many of their problems or mishaps. As a singer, sharing melodious tunes throughout the day.

An actor, who plays many roles and many parts in different peoples lives.

There are many parts to me to help me grow as a person and also to help others grow and learn about themselves and to help them achieve all the goals and many

Successes in their lives.

Remember Me   **September 1995**

Remember the times we shared?
The smiles that greeted us as we passed by?
Remember our talks and the way we laughed?
Sometimes even the way we cried?
Remember the long walks home and the rainy days?
Remember when you needed help, and I put forth my hand?
Remember the silly jokes? Remember me as your friend?
When I promised you I would always be around?
Remember the pact we made? To always be there for one another?
Remember to enjoy life and all those who enter it.
Remember your brothers and sisters and the ones who look out for you.
Remember God and all He has done for you.
And when you remember all the good things in your life past and present,
Don't' forget to…..Remember Me!

Born To Die   **April 1995**

You were born just to die.
Every minute, every second, you are getting closer to dying.
So while on this earth, why not do something positive with your life?
What does your life mean? Will you help your brothers and sisters along the way?
Will you be a primary example for others to follow along or will you cop out by giving back negative standards, such as drugs, murderers, thieves, killings, suicide?
Why die miserable when you can die knowing that you can make a difference in someone else's life? Remember, the race is not given to the swift, neither is it given to the strong, but to him that endures to the very end!

Why?   **June 1994**

Sometimes I wonder why things are the way they are.
Why so many innocent people get killed.
Why innocent babies suffer the impact of death.
Why nobody respects others, even themselves.
Why racial tension is constantly passed on from generation to generation.
Why hatred is such a physical act, rather than just a spoken word.
Why there isn't any equal justice for anybody, for our people.
Why are gangs such a way of life now?
Why do we want to push the world into coming to and end faster than it should?
Why?

What Is A Friend?   **August 1995**

Someone you meet who connects with you,
Mind, Body, Soul, and Spirit.
Someone who understands you.
Someone who stands by your side.
Walks with you hand in hand.
Someone who corrects you when you're wrong,
But yet will stand in your defense.
Someone who encourages, uplifts, speaks his mind.
Can keep your secrets with a dying honor never to reveal them.
Gives you a crying shoulder to lean on.
Will support you in anything you choose to do.
Someone who will see you through to the very end of life's turmoils.
A true friend is someone who will never let you down.
Friends are forever.

When I Grow Up   **September 1995**

When I Grow Up,
I want to have left behind a legacy and a history of the most important aspects of life: To Live, To Love, and To Grow.

When I Grow Up,
I want my parents to see what they have produced was a boy growing up into a responsible young man, strong and capable of handling all of his responsibilities.

When I Grow Up,
I want to set the pace for my other siblings, as they look at me and strive not to be like me, but to be better than me. To know that within themselves, they can do and become whatever they choose to become as young adults.

When I Grow Up,
I want my friends to envy the achievements as far as trying to build a successful career and becoming the man for the future.

When I Grow Up,
I want my wife to look at me and say, "I am proud that out of all the men in this world, I chose the one who is going to set the pace for others to follow in being a successful businessman, husband and wonderful father".

When I Grow Up,
I want my children to be proud of their father who is constantly working hard to make the way a better one for his children, who can follow in their father's footsteps in achieving their goals and dreams for the future.

When I Grow Up,
I want the world to be proud of the man who has set the pace for what today's young men should be like: Responsible, In Control, and never lacking knowledge to survive in a society run by ignorance.

Patience   **December 1995**

Sometimes it's hard to wait.
Sometimes we jump the gun.
We run ahead of ourselves.
We don't take the time out to think about the consequences, once we set the pace to do it ourselves…..Patience.

But if we trust in God, and know in due time that everything He said in His word,
Everything He promised us, will come to pass, then we have won the race that is set before us……Patience.

It's not for our bad, but for our good to continue to wait until our change comes.
And when our change comes, we rejoice, for God doeth all things well.
Miraculously, infinitely, and according to the promise He has given us.
Our patience is the key that allows God to open every door…..Patience.

You Can Make It If You Try   **January 1996**

Sometimes he smiles and the world is a wonderful place to live in.
Sometimes he is sad, and it seems as though his world has come to an end.
What's going on inside of his head?
What makes him laugh? What makes him cry?
Where are his friends? Does anyone care?

What are his thoughts? What are his goals?
Does he plan to excel? Does he want to succeed?
Does he believe in himself? Does he believe he can make it?
Stop and say to yourself, "In spite of it all, I Can, I Will, I Shall!"

Don't stop! Don't give up! Don't give in! Don't give out!
Believe you can and you will.
Believe you can win, and you've reached your heart's contentment.
Believe the old saying, "You Can Make It, If You Try!"

God Gave Me You (A Tribute to My Mother, Mrs. Joyce Mattox) October 1995

God gave me you, to help see me through.
When I had lost my way, you never stopped, you continued to pray.
When I wanted to give up, you prayed "Lord fill his cup",
And that made my joy, full.

Because you were faithful to the cause
When others turned their backs, God is, because,
You have been chosen, His light shines on you.
God is pleased, He will see you through.
There's never been a time and there's never been a day,
You let much get by, without wanting to pray.
And just because you mean what you say, and mean what you do,
In His own knowledge and meaning,
God Gave Me You!

Heaven (A Tribute to My Grandparents, The Gray's)   **December 1995**

You were my second parents.
You taught me all the things there was to know about honesty, love and loyalty.
You taught me what was right, and never allowed me to forget when I had done wrong. You brought me to church and taught me "The Fear of God", and how to keep His commandments. You taught me to respect my elders.
And to never sass grown-ups. Or even act unseemly.
You showed me how much fun I could have with my peers and "older people".
You spoiled me with nice gifts, and always had time to cook some good ole down home food. You always kept me in your prayers, and before God.
You never hesitated to "whip" me when I needed it.
You always had an encouraging word to help me make it through the day.
You always had time for your family.
And when division set in, you did not hesitate to make peace.
Your light shines in all of us.
And even though down here on earth you are missed,
I know for a fact, I'll share a seat next to you,
When I get into…..HEAVEN.

In His Shadow   **January 1996**

Somehow I feel I already know you.
That somehow we've met.
That our spirits have somehow connected with one another.
We are similar in a lot of ways.
It's almost like we were brothers.
Our moods, our actions, our thoughts are so much alike. Were we related?
Could you have been my twin?

Why didn't we meet? Why haven't we talked?
We would have gotten along well I believed.
You would have been the headstrong one.
I would have been the sensitive calm one.
We would have argued most of the time, but yet remained close.
But now you're gone to a place with no worries or cares.
You are missed now, missed down here.
Friends, family, loved ones, even me.
Someone you've never met, sitting here…..In Your Shadow!
Sleep Peacefully.

(In Loving Memory of Aaron Kelly)

Black Unity (A Tribute to Black Rap Artists) November 1995

With a tune in mind and a pen in my hand,
Writing true lyrics is where I take command.
My goal is set high and my aim is never low,
My skills tell the story, I am true to flow.

I want to share with you my round-the-way beat,
That makes you clap your hands and makes you move your feet.
It's not a simple pleasure, nor a common gesture,
To make you get with the groove and stay in the mood.
So tell your friends and loved ones we're here to stay,
We'll never back down, we'll never run away.
As long as we're here, we'll share the flow,
We'll stand together, we'll steal the show.
With one common goal we have set in our minds,
To take over the world with our grooves and our rhymes.

I PLEDGE ALLEGIANCE TO GOD   August 1993

I PLEDGE ALLEGIANCE TO GOD,
THE ALMIGHTY CREATOR OF ALL THINGS GIVEN TO THE UNIVERSE.
THE CREATOR OF LAND, SKY, AND SEA.
THE STARS, THE MOON, AND THE SUN.
FOR ALL ANIMALS, GREAT AND SMALL.
FOR THE CREATION OF MAN AND WOMAN,
BOTH CREATED IN GOD'S OWN IMAGE.
ALL ALLEGIANCE GOES TO GOD.

I PLEDGE ALLEGIANCE TO GOD,
FOR SENDING HIS OWN SON TO DIE.
FOR THE BLOOD THAT WAS SHED FROM THE CROSS ON HIGH.
FOR HIS SAVING GRACE, THROUGHOUT THE HUMAN RACE.
ALL ALLEGIANCE GOES TO GOD.

I PLEDGE ALLEGIANCE TO GOD, FOR I KNOW HE'S ALWAYS THERE.
FOR WHEN LIFE'S STORMS ARE RAGING, AND WHEN THE BILLOWS ROLL,
WHEN I FEEL AS THOUGH I HAVE NO CONTROL,
AND THEN GOD STEPS IN.
I PLEDGE ALLEGIANCE, BECAUSE HE WILL NEVER LEAVE ME ALONE.
ALTHOUGH AT TIMES I MAY FEEL LIKE NO ONE CARES, NO ONE TO COUNT ON.
BUT GOD IS ALWAYS THERE.
HE'S THAT KIND OF FRIEND, TO COME AND SEE ABOUT ME.
HE LET'S ME KNOW THAT HE IS THE BEST THING THAT EVER HAPPENED TO ME.
HE IS A TRUE FRIEND, UNTIL THE END.
AND THAT'S WHY.....I PLEDGE ALLEGIANCE TO GOD!

Life   **April 1995**

Some people love, while others hate.
Some people laugh, while others cry.
Some enjoy their lives, while others suffer misery and pain.
Some accomplish their goals in life, while others just live from hand to mouth.
Some marry their soul mate, while others just live alone.
Some are happy, others sad.
Some people are rich, while others are poor.
Some walk tall, while others step low.
Let's face it, everybody's life is not the same.

Depression   **April 1995**

I had a series of depressions.
I always had a low self-esteem about myself.
I always thought I was unattractive.
That looks were more important than personality, then integrity, than morals.
I felt like everyone around me didn't like me for whatever reason.
I always felt there was something wrong with me.
Even to a point I felt God didn't love me.
I became suicidal, planning each and every step into ending my life.
I literally felt worthless.
But one day I overcame depression.
I decided that my life was too valuable to end it.
That it was not meant to drown in sorrow.
I somehow overcame the negativity of my life and picked myself up again.
I told myself everyday that I was somebody, instead of a nobody.
That I had inner beauty, that somehow my life meant something and I made a difference in this world.
That depression was only a state of mind, not a state of being!

www.ingramcontent.com/pod-product-compliance
Lightning Source LLC
Chambersburg PA
CBHW032212040426
42449CB00005B/557